400 Years

Prayer, Praise, Protest and White Justice

A 30 Day Black Lives Matters Prayer Devotional

Dr. Imelda Hunt Ph.D.

400 Years
Prayer, Praise, Protest and White Justice: *A 30 Day*
Black Lives Matters Prayer Devotional

Editing & Formatting by: *Pieces of Me Publications, LLC*
Number: 419-322-0438
Email: msharmonyus@yahoo.com

TABLE OF CONTENTS

Acknowledgements

First and foremost, all thanks to our loving God and His angels who have watched over me my entire life. Thanks to my daughters' Gisella Hunt Oliver, Nikki N. Hunt, my grandchildren, Ashlei and Michael Carpenter, and my sisters and brothers for their understanding by giving me the time to complete this book, to teach, and to fulfill my purpose without being resentful. I greatly appreciate the teachings and fellowship of Bishop Pastor Patricia McKinstry, my church family at Worship Center in Toledo, Ohio and Latoya Williams who also helped to edit this book. I am profoundly grateful for the friendship of Eddie Allen, Jr. and Milton T. Hunt. I am thankful for the support of the Department of Africology and African American Studies faculty and staff and my students at Eastern Michigan University.

Introduction

This devotional was written to bless and support the people who are in the streets choosing to make a difference. It is also written to support African Americans who are moved by the injustices that have lasted more than 400 years against African Americans. This devotional can be used as a guide to seek liberation, peace, justice, equality and righteousness through prayers of intercession for African Americans. This is not a new cry and many of the devotional entries are inspired by the 400 years of African American struggle by leaders like Dr. Martin Luther King Jr., Ella Baker, Marcus Garvey, Nat Turner, etc. Finally, these prayers are from the Holy Bible and are confirmed in the Word of God.

"Lest we forget" as we go about our daily lives that this struggle for basic necessitate such as healthcare, a fair living wage, an inclusive education for black children, and fair housing is denied to a majority of African American people in this country and people of color in other places in the world. This should not be so in the land of plenty and in a land where others are so privileged to have obtained these benefits through injustice and racism. This inequality began with the ideals of democracy that all men are equal while denying the humanity of others based on the color of their skin which gave whites an unequal distribution of wealth and advantages for 400 years. In a land that believes in the

Holy Word of God these inequities are no longer acceptable.

I encourage you, as we take to the streets, march to Washington, and participate at the polls, let us not forget God who commands us to ask. By remembering these examples of prayers and scriptures, I hope God grants you the ability to stand and fight the good fight of faith. Speak truth to power. Pray and cry out to God so His promises come to pass.

Day One

Scripture:

"If my people, which are called by my name, shall humble themselves and pray, and seek your face, and turn from our wicked ways; then will you hear from heaven and forgive our sin and will heal our land.

2 Chronicles 7:14

"But the LORD said, 'What have you done? Listen! Your brother's blood cries out to me from the ground!'"

Genesis 4:10, <u>NLT</u>

<u>Inspirational Commentary</u>

W.E.B. Dubois (1863-1968) often called the "Father of African American Culture," and the first African American PHD to graduate from the University of Harvard prayed about his times as an activist and leader of the National Association for the Advancement of Colored People (NAACP). Dubois's prayer which follows, references Queen Esther in the old testament of the Bible who was praying for her people:

~Prayer~

"Give us grace, O God, to dare to do the deed which we well know cries to be done. Let us not hesitate because of ease, or the words of men's

mouths, or our own lives. Mighty causes are calling us—the freeing of women, the training of children, the putting down of hate and murder and poverty— all these and more. But they call with voices that mean work and sacrifices and death. Mercifully grant us, O God, the spirit of Esther, that we say: I will go unto the King and if I perish, I perish."

Great men and women of God have not failed to address and ask God to help them to overcome the violence and cruelty to their people. Clearly, we can and must do the same. Prayer is a force that touches eternal power. Prayer requires the body, soul, and spirit. Prayer is a holistic experience.

Voices

"I can't breathe, man. Please." ... George Floyd, 2020

Day Two

Scripture:

"Let justice roll like a river and righteousness like a never-failing stream."

Amos 5:24

<u>Inspirational Commentary</u>

Mary McLeod Bethune (1875-1955) an activist requested that 'If I have a legacy to leave my people, it is my philosophy of living and serving." She was an accomplished teacher and speaker for women's rights who served and founded the Daytona Normal and National Industrial Institute for Negro Girls in 1904. Her prayer below is an inclusive world prayer for others. It acknowledges God's love and wish that the justice that has been denied to African Americans in this country will not be denied to them or to others.

~Prayer~

Father, we call Thee Father because we love Thee. We are glad to be called Thy children, and to dedicate our lives to the service that extends through willing hearts and hands to the betterment of all mankind. We send a cry of

Thanksgiving for people of all races, creeds, classes, and colors the world over, and pray that through the instrumentality of our lives the spirit of peace, joy, fellowship, and brotherhood shall circle the world. We know that this world is filled with discordant notes, but help us, Father, to so unite our efforts that we may all join in one harmonious symphony for peace and brotherhood, justice, and equality of opportunity for all men. The tasks performed today with forgiveness for all our errors, we dedicate, dear Lord, to Thee. Grant us strength and courage and faith and humility sufficient for the tasks assigned to us.

The task at hand may not reflect the past but be reflected in the determination by which this generation of African Americans has set out to change America's injustices to create a "new normal." Let us who believe in them cry out to God until we see God's normal, and not a white justice, but a Godly justice.

Voices

"There he is." Moses Wright answers as a witness in the courtroom to the death of Emmitt Till.

Day Three

Scripture:
"Therefore all they that devour thee shall be devoured; and all thine adversaries, every one of them, shall go into captivity; and they that spoil thee shall be a spoil, and all that prey upon thee will I give for a prey."

Jeremiah 30:16

<u>Inspirational Commentary</u>
Marcus Garvey (1887-1940) was born in Jamaica and was the leader of the United Negro Improvement Association (UNIA) and African Communities League. Under Garvey's leadership in New York, blacks owned ships, newspapers, developed economic empowerment plans and a vision for African Americans to return to Africa. Garvey, like many African American leaders during his time, was known as a race man. During his imprisonment in Atlanta, his first speech to blacks in the diaspora was a recognition of God's power in his life.

~Prayer~

Garvey said, "Look for me in the whirlwind or the storm, look for me all around you, for, with God's grace, I shall come and bring with me countless millions of black slaves who have died in America and the West Indies and the millions in Africa to aid you in the fight for Liberty, Freedom, and Life.

Garvey is recognized by many historians as the leader who had the largest following of African Americans in history and one of the first Pan-Africanist.

Voices

"Kenneth Chamberlain, 66 "Why do you have your guns out?"

Day Four

Scripture:

"Oh, that my head were a spring of water and my eyes a fountain of tears! I would weep day and night for the slain of my people."

Jeremiah 9:1

<u>Inspirational Commentary</u>

Ella Baker (1903-1986) was an activist and organizer during the civil rights movement. She also mentored other activists including Student Nonviolence Coordinating Committee (SNCC) leader, Stokely (Kwame Ture) Carmichael. A servant-leader, Baker believed that it was important to develop. . .the individual to his highest potential for the benefit of the group. Often considered a woman "behind the scenes" and an unsung hero, she organized and supported Martin Luther King Jr., women's rights, and mass incarceration organizations.

She is quoted here:

"The major job was getting people to understand that they had something within their power that they could use, and it could only be used if they understood what was happening and how group action could counter violence. To me young people come first. They have the courage where we fail. And if I can shed some light as they carry us through the gale... Struggling myself don't mean a

whole lot I come to realize. That teaching others to stand up and fight is the only way my struggle survives."

Although Baker did not remain someone who you would think of as the everyday person, she began as someone who saw a need and filled whatever need she could. Praying the scriptures above and in this devotional is also fulfilling a need and God's call to pray.

Voices
Amadou Diallo, 23 "Mom, I'm going to college."

Day Five

Scripture:

"Listen to me, my people; hear me, my nation: Instruction will go out from me; my justice will become a light to the nations. My righteousness draws near speedily, my salvation is on the way, and my arm will bring justice to the nations. The islands will look to me and wait in hope for my arm.

Isaiah 51:4-5

<u>Inspirational Commentary</u>

Harriet Tubman (1820-1913) was called "Moses" because she led so many enslaved Africans to freedom through the Underground Railroad. Freedom to her included the liberation of others. Her faith in God was her strength. This was her declaration to God, "I'm going to hold steady on You, an' You've got to see me through."

Thomas Garrett said of Tubman, "I never met any person of any color who had more confidence in the voice of God." Tubman prayed (paraphrased):

So it was with me. I had crossed the line of which I had so long been dreaming. I was free; but there was no one to welcome me to the land of freedom, I was a stranger in a strange land, and my home after all was down in the old cabin quarter, with the old folks, and my brothers and sisters. But to this solemn resolution I came; I was free, and they should be free also; I would make a home for them in the North, and the Lord helping me, I would bring them all there. Oh, how I prayed then, lying all alone on the cold damp ground:

~Prayer~

'Oh, dear Lord', I said. I haven't got no friend but you. Come to my help Lord, for I'm in trouble!

Her ability to see the needs of others and her reliance on God gives us another picture of the type of courage and strength that will make Black Lives Matter Movement personal today. Jeremiah the biblical prophet also saw the needs of other as if they were his own children. God answered him in the scriptures. We can pray today and ask of God and He promised in the scripture to hear us.

Voices

Trayvon Martin, 16 "What are you following me for?"

Day Six

Scripture:

"My eyes fail from weeping, I am in torment within; my heart is poured out on the ground because my people are destroyed because children and infants faint in the streets of the city."

Lam 2:11

<u>Inspirational Commentary</u>

Coretta Scott King (1927-2006) was an activist, organizer and wife of Dr. Martin Luther King Jr. She was also a mother who had to raise her children in a time when daily her family was the target of public hatred. Today Dr. King's legacy has been glorified which pacify the hatred and bitterness that he faced as one of the leaders of Civil Rights Movement. We must not ignore the courage that Coretta and his children experienced. This is a public prayer that she prayed:

~Prayer~

Eternal and everlasting God, who art the Father of all mankind, as we turn aside from the hurly-burly of everyday living, may our hearts and souls, yea our very spirits, be lifted upward to
Thee, for it is from Thee that all blessing cometh. Keep us ever mindful of our dependence upon Thee,

for without Thee our efforts are but naught. We pray for Thy divine guidance as we travel the highways of life. We pray for more courage. We pray for more faith and above all we pray for more love. May we somehow come to understand the true meaning of Thy love as revealed to us in the life, death and resurrection of Thy son and our Lord and Master, Jesus Christ. May the Cross ever remind us of Thy great love, for greater love no man hath given. This is our supreme example, O God. May we be constrained to follow in the name and spirit of Jesus, we pray.

The wisdom of Mrs. King's prayer speaks to our everyday experiences with racism and how we can defeat the toll that it tries to take on our daily life. Her example in prayer can provide us with strength for the journey in this time and the days to come. We know that the power of our prayers comes from the word of God and His promises. We should pray those words which is ultimately the purpose of this devotional.

Voice

Rodney King. "Can't we all just get along?"

Day Seven

Scripture :

"They will come and shout for joy on the heights of Zion; they will rejoice in the bounty of the Lord— the grain, the new wine and the olive oil, the young of the flocks and herds. They will be like a well-watered garden, and they will sorrow no more."

Jeremiah 31:12

<u>Inspirational Commentary</u>

Ida B. Wells (1862-1931) was a journalist, educator, and civil rights activist. She fought daily against the violence suffered by African Americans at the hands of white people by posting the number of daily lynching of African Americans outside her newspaper building and published those stories and other atrocities in her newspaper. She said, "In slave times the Negro was kept subservient and submissive by the frequency and severity of the scourging, but, with freedom, a new system of intimidation came into vogue; the Negro was not only whipped and scourged; he was killed.

Eric Gerard Pearman writes that Ida B. Wells was an uncompromising crusader in her relentless pursuit of social justice and racial uplift. He concludes that it was her exposure to the traditions of biblical truths in the African American evangelical experience, which focuses on social justice and liberation themes depicted by old testament prophets and the new testament ministry of Jesus Christ that contributed to these characteristics. Ida B. Wells was a church member.

Voices

John Crawford, 22 "It's not real."

Day Eight

Scripture:

"Then Jesus told his disciples a parable to show them that they should always pray and not give up. 2 He said: "In a certain town there was a judge who neither feared God nor cared what people thought. 3 And there was a widow in that town who kept coming to him with the plea, 'Grant me justice against my adversary.' "For some time he refused. But finally he said to himself, 'Even though I don't fear God or care what people think, yet because this widow keeps bothering me, I will see that she gets justice, so that she won't eventually come and attack me!' " And the Lord said, "Listen to what the unjust judge says. And will not God bring about justice for his chosen ones, who cry out to him day and night? Will he keep putting them off? I tell you, he will see that they get justice, and quickly. However, when the Son of Man comes, will he find faith on the earth?"

Luke 18:1-8

Inspirational Commentary

Fannie Lou Hammer (1917-1977) a civil rights activist. She was not a school educated woman, but she debated many who were.

Her speeches were an acknowledgement to God. She challenged her community and others, *"The spirit of the*

Lord is upon me because he has anointed me to preach the gospel to the poor. He has sent me to heal the brokenhearted, to preach deliverance to the captive . . . to set at liberty to them who are bruised, to preach the acceptable year of the Lord (Luke 4:18)." Hammer was addressing the Delta's at a freedom rally in 1963.

~Prayer~

Hammer appealed to God, "I have asked God, I said, 'Now Lord'—and you have too— ain't no need to lie and say that you ain't," she admonished those who might outwardly scoff at her desperate plea. "Said, 'Open a way for us.' Said, 'Please make a way for us, Jesus . . . where I can stand up and speak for my race and speak for these hungry children.' And he opened a way.

Her ability to tell the truth plainly and her determination to see things change was a great asset to the Civil Rights Movement. She said, "With the people, for the people, by the people. I crack up when I hear it; I say, with the handful, for the handful, by the handful, 'cause that's what really happens." How often have we all sat back and let a few do the fighting for us?

Voices

"Justice is what love looks like in public." Cornel West.

Day Nine

Scripture:

"Yet the LORD longs to be gracious to you; therefore he will rise up to show you compassion. For the LORD is a God of justice. Blessed are all who wait for him! People of Zion, who live in Jerusalem, you will weep no more. How gracious he will be when you cry for help! As soon as he hears, he will answer you."

Isaiah 30:18-19

<u>Inspirational Commentary</u>

Martin Luther King Jr. (1929-1968) espoused a doctrine of nonviolence which fueled the civil rights movement of the 60s. However, towards the end of his life King realized that it was systemic racism and injustices in America that needed his attention. The prayer that he prayed here is especially inspiring for many African Americans in the church who have gained some small privileges from the system. Revisiting King's prayer can refocus and re-center our purpose.

~Prayer~

"O Thou Eternal God, out of whose absolute power and infinite intelligence the whole universe has come into being, we humbly confess that we have not loved thee with our hearts, souls and minds, and

we have not loved our neighbors as Christ loved us. We have all too often lived by our own selfish impulses rather than by the life of sacrificial love as revealed by Christ. We often give in order to receive. We love our friends and hate our enemies. We go the first mile but dare not travel the second. We forgive but dare not forget. And so as we look within ourselves, we are confronted with the appalling fact that the history of our lives is the history of an eternal revolt against you. But thou, O God, have mercy upon us. Forgive us for what we could have been but failed to be. Give us the intelligence to know your will. Give us the courage to do your will. Give us the devotion to love thy will. In the name and spirit of Jesus we pray. Amen."

The writing and teaching of the history of African Americans in this country has been skewed. Basically, the history is told to support the prevailing system of injustices against African Americans, all people of color and poor people. King's legacy studied, reminds us to pray, to march and to fight these inequalities.

Voices

Eric Garner, 43 "I can't breathe."

Day Ten

Scripture:

"Lord let them be confounded that persecutes our families and let not our families be confounded, let our enemies be dismayed but let not our families be dismayed. Bring upon our enemies the day of evil and destroy them with double destruction in Jesus name."

Jeremiah 17:18

<u>Inspirational Commentary</u>

Nat Turner (1800-1831) a prophet and a preacher who believed in God's word. He was often seen praying, fasting, and studying the Bible. He believed the Bible was not just for plantation owners but all people especially for the enslaved African. Believing that God was no respect of person he led enslaved Africans with his knowledge of the Bible to fight back. He is credited with having led the most successful slave rebellion. Although considered a rebel by white slave owners, he defined his and his people's freedom through a God given omen. Justice and freedom were not one-way streets. Turner explained: "As I was praying one day at my plough, the spirit spoke to me, saying, "Seek ye the kingdom of heaven and all things shall be added unto you."

There were many other men in the history of the early African's enslaved in America who studied the Bible and were also religious leaders, like Denmark Vessey, and

Gabriel Posser, a blacksmith, who led a rebellion. 400 years of various instruments of protest are behind us. How will we stand against these injustices today?

Voices

Oscar Grant, 22 "You shot me! You shot me!"

Day Eleven

Scripture:

"Is not this the kind of fasting I have chosen: to loose the chains of injustice and untie the cords of the yoke, to set the oppressed free and break every yoke?"

Isaiah 58:6

<u>Inspirational Commentary</u>

Sojourner Truth (1797-1883) although she did not find her faith sitting in the pews or on an altar in the church, Sojourner Truth had faith and passion for God. She became a member of a segregated Kingston's St. James Methodist Episcopal Church in 1827 where her public ministry began. She considered herself a friend of God. Her prayer for freedom for her son and other enslaved Africans, and women are filled with passion.

~Prayer~

"Do For Me God" . . .*Oh, God, you know I have no money, but you can make the people do for me, and you must make the people do for me. I will never give you peace till you do, God."*

Voices

George Floyd 46, *"Stop I can't breathe..."* Minnesota 2020

Day Twelve

Scripture:

"We know that you Lord is able to do exceedingly abundantly above all that we are asking and thinking concerning our families, according to the power that now worketh in us."

Ephesians 3: 20

<u>Inspirational Commentary</u>

Frederick Douglass born into slavery escaped from his owner's plantation to freedom. He was a self-taught orator and leader of African Americans. He also fought for the liberation of women from the tyranny of a patriarchal government. In his famous autobiography, *Up from Slavery*, he wrestles with the ideal of justice. His prayers, "In Search of Freedom" follows:

~Prayer~

"You are loosed from your moorings and are free; I am fast in my chains and am a slave! You move merrily before the gentle gale and I sadly before the bloody whip! You are freedom's swift-winged angels that fly round the world; I am confined in bands of iron! O that I were free! O, that I were on one of your gallant decks, and under your protecting wing! Alas! Betwixt me

and you, the turbid waters roll. Go on, go on. O that I could also go! Could I but swim! If I could fly! O, why was I born a man, of whom to make a brute! The glad ship is gone; she hides in the dim distance. I am left in the hottest hell of unending slavery. O God, save me! God deliver me! Let me be free! Is there any God? Why am I a slave? I will run away. I will not stand it. Get caught or get clear. I'll try it. I had as well die with ague as the fever. I have only one life to lose. I had as well be killed running as die standing. Only think of it; one hundred miles straight north, and I am free! Yes! God helping me, I will."

Douglass remains one of America's most famous orators. His freedom as we witnessed above was obtained through his crying out in petitions and prayers to God. His escape to freedom was not obtained overnight but he fought in prayer.

Voices

Michael Brown 18, *"I don't have a gun. Stop shooting."*

Day Thirteen

Scripture:

"The Lord Almighty is with us; the God of Jacob is our fortress."

Psalm 46:7

"Do not be afraid of them; the Lord your God himself will fight for you."

Deuteronomy 3:22

<u>Inspirational Commentary</u>

Martin Robison Delany (1812 –1885) was an African American abolitionist, journalist, physician, soldier and writer. He has been considered by most, "The Father of Black Nationalism." and arguably the first proponent of black nationalism. His vision and prayers are illustrated in the following passage:

~Prayer~

> *"We must be willing, because it is as contrary to nature as the blending is as light to darkness, to cease looking to Providence to do that for us which God has given us the ability and means to do for ourselves. God works by means and not by miracles. He has placed within our means for the accomplishment of certain ends; the application of*

these means will attain the end aimed at or desired."

Early African American leaders like Delaney were very conscious of God and the power of prayer. They had a balanced vision of prayer and purpose which we can look back and learn from. Sankofa, an African proverb to go back and retrieve is likewise another call to use the past to draw wisdom.

Voices

"Get off of him, now." Another bystander said, *"Bro he's not moving." As police office Derek Chauvin keeps his knee on George Floyd's neck for 8 minutes and 46 seconds until Floyd goes into cardiac arrest and later dies.*

Day Fourteen

Scripture:

"Turn from evil and do good; then you will dwell in the land forever. For the LORD loves the just and will not forsake his faithful ones. Wrongdoers will be completely destroyed; the offspring of the wicked will perish. The righteous will inherit the land and dwell in it forever."

Psalm 37:27-29

<u>Inspirational Commentary</u>

David Walker (1796-1830) was an activist, abolitionist, and writer. He wrote during the abolitionist's movement, *An Appeal to the Coloured Citizens of the World.* Like others, African American leaders including Dubois, Garvey and Walker also had a Pan-African sensibility. In Walker's Appeal he wrote:

"We coloured people of these United States, our the most degraded, wretched, and abject set of beings that ever lived since the world began, and I pray God, that none like us ever may live until time shall be no more. They tell us of the Israelites in Egypt, the <u>Helots</u> in Sparta, and of the Roman slaves whose sufferings under those ancient and heathen nations, were, in comparison with ours, under this enlightened and Christian nation, no more than a <u>cypher</u>. Or in other words, those heathen nations of antiquity had but little more among them than the name and form of

slavery; while wretchedness and endless miseries were reserved, apparently in a phial, to be poured out upon our fathers, ourselves, and our children by Christian Americans."

"It fell upon blacks, he argued, to reject the notion that the Bible sanctioned slavery and urge whites to repent before God could punish them for their wickedness. He continues in *Walker's Appeal in Four Articles*, "There is great work for you to do... You have to prove to the Americans and the world that we are *men*, and not brutes, as we have been represented, and by millions treated. Remember, to let the aim of your labors among your brethren, and particularly the youths, be the dissemination of education and religion."

Voices

"You feeling good about yourself? You feel good about yourself? You feel good about yourself, don't you? For a failure to signal...Why am I being arrested? Can you tell me that part? Are you ... kidding?" Excerpt of Sandra Bland's Traffic Stop.

Day Fifteen

Scripture:

"For there is no respect of persons with God."

Romans 12:11

<u>Inspirational Commentary</u>

London Ferrill, also spelled Ferrell, **(1789–1854)** was a former <u>slave</u> and carpenter from Virginia. His wife, a free black, purchased his freedom and they moved to. Kentucky in 1812. However, some sources believed that Ferrill was given his freedom by his slave owner, Colonel Samuel Overton, when he died. Ferrill became the second preacher of the First African Baptist Church in Lexington, Kentucky, serving from 1823 to 1854. During his 31 years of service, Ferrill attracted and baptized many new members in the growing region. By 1850 the church had 1,820 members and was the largest of any congregation in the state, black or white. His love for people is demonstrated in his last prayer.

~Prayer~

"God, bless the Church of which I am pastor ... and grant that it may continue to prosper and do good among the colored race. And, merciful Father! bless the white people, who have always

treated me as though I was a white man, and bless ... the Church of Christ everywhere--bless Christians in every land--bless O, Lord!"

Like Ferrill, many men and women ministers of God today, experience the same respect from both the black and white race. Let us pray for their continued success and understanding."

Voices

"Put your hands out to the side." ---Officer Adam Coy, within seconds, backs off before firing his weapon, striking, 47 years old, African American male, Andre Maurice Hill. Hill died at the hospital just before 2:30 a.m. Hill was not guilty of any crime. No weapon was recovered at the scene.

~ Yusuf Dubois Davis Abdul Lateef~

Day Sixteen

Scripture:

"This is what the Lord Almighty said, Administer true justice; show mercy and compassion to one another. [10] Do not oppress the widow or the fatherless, the foreigner or the poor. Do not plot evil against each other."

Zechariah 7:9-10

Inspirational Commentary

Bethany Veney (1815-1916) born a slave authored *The Narrative of Bethany Veney, a Slave Woman* in 1889, over twenty years after slavery was abolished. In her chapter "Religious Experiences" she explains her conversion and faith. In the final chapter of her slave narrative, she writes that:

"I am now, at seventy-four years of age, the owner and occupant of a small house at 21 Tufts Street, Worcester, Mass. My daughter and family are near me, in an adjoining house, also owned by me. I have three grandchildren living. My back is not so straight nor so strong, my sight is not so clear, nor my limbs so nimble as they once were; but I am still ready and glad to do whatsoever my hand findeth to do, waiting only for the call to "come up higher"."

Veney's narrative summarizes what it was like to live a life of faith and courage during those years of her enslavement. She believed in her religion. Forbidden by some of her slave owners to worship or go to camp meetings, she went when she could. Veney was rewarded with strength and character. She is an example of humility and an "overcoming faith."

Voices

Daniel Prude 44. "they're trying to kill me. . ." NY. 2020

Day Seventeen

Scripture:

"I said to myself, God will bring into judgment both the righteous and the wicked, for there will be a time for every activity, a time to judge every deed."

Ecclesiastes 3:17

<u>Inspirational Commentary</u>

Shirley Chisholm (1924-2005) was a politician from New York. In 1972, she became the first Black American and the first woman to run for the Democratic Party presidential nomination. She also served seven terms in Congress. When asked how she wished to be remembered, Chisholm replied:

"When I die, I want to be remembered as a woman who lived in the 20th century and who dared to be a catalyst of change. I don't want to be remembered as the first Black woman who went to Congress. And I don't even want to be remembered as the first woman who happened to be Black to make the bid for the presidency," she said.

"I want to be remembered as a woman who fought for change in the 20th century, that's what I want." When I read the lessons that she inspires, two quotes from her book, "Unbought and Unbossed" are among the most revealing and persistent problems today. Her first quote,

"When <u>morality</u> comes up against <u>profit</u>, it is seldom that profit loses." Also, the second quote, "The difference between de jure and de facto segregation is the difference between open, forthright <u>bigotry</u> and the shamefaced kind that works through unwritten agreements between real estate dealers, school officials, and local politicians. Her last observations are some of the most subtle and disguised strategies of systemic racism. If we are, in fact as a people, to lift ourselves up by our own bootstraps, how if deals are made behind our backs to cut the straps? We must be vigilante. Prayer and systemic changes are a few steps that can heal these injustices.

Voices

"Who's there?... Breonna Taylor, a 26-year-old EMT, was shot eight times after police broke down the door to her apartment.

Day Eighteen

Scripture:

"It is joy to the just to do judgement: but destruction shall be to the workers of iniquity"

Proverbs 21: 15

<u>Inspirational Commentary</u>

Charles Cobb Jr writes in his book, "On the Road to Freedom: A Guided Tour," about the African presence in St. Augustine Florida. A town established in 1565 where some of the first Africans in America settled and help build San Marco Fort to fight the British. San Marco was also a refuge for the enslave African run away from the British colonies. San Moses, the first settlement of free blacks in America was established two miles from San Marco in 1738. After the Civil War, a black community called Africa was established and is now called Lincolnville Historic District. The perseverance of early Africa in the Americas is amazing.

The state of Florida and other cities have countless experiences and a history of many civil rights events which African Americans extraordinary participated in to build the united states of America. Our young African American children's frustration exemplifies these omissions in the history books, courts, employment, and laws. Our present Black Lives Matter Movement speaks to these systemic ills. Education at its best should empower all Americans not just the history of Europeans.

Voices

Elijah J. McClain, "I can't breathe." He was 23 years old and died in a choke hold by a police officer in 1996.

Day Nineteen

Scripture:

"Praise ye the Lord. Blessed is the man that fears the Lord, that delights greatly in his commandments."

Psalm 112:1

<u>Inspirational Commentary</u>

Apartheid was a system of government in South Africa that lessen the rights of the majority of Africans and gave rights and rule to the British white minorities. This system toppled after many years by the people of South Africa and leaders like Nelson and Winnie Mandela. Bishop Desmond Tutu, named the first black archbishop of Cape Town South Africa in 1956, said, "We don't want apartheid liberalized. We want it dismantled. You can't improve something that is intrinsically evil." Apartheid has been described as a man wanting sovereignty for his own people in land that is not his own by denying the inhabitants their rights. While many of apartheid's strongholds damaged African people's efforts to unify into a united Africa, South Africa is no longer under British rule. Tutu, a leader for justice also said of the church, that [it] … has a responsibility for all, the rich and the poor, the ruler and the ruled, the oppressed and the oppressor, but it needs to point out that God does take sides. Incredibly, he sides with those whom the world would marginalize, whom the world considers of little account.

Are Christians not to believe that black children will be mighty in this land? Or are we believing the media stereotypes that only black middle class children who represent whiteness are the only ones who deserve greatness. Or are we believing God?

Voices

"Father forgive them; for they know not what they do." Jesus (Luke 23:34).

Day Twenty

Scripture:

"Whoever says to the guilty, "You are innocent," will be cursed by peoples and denounced by nations. But it will go well with those who convict the guilty, and rich blessing will come on them."

Proverbs 24:24-25

<u>Inspirational Commentary</u>

Under **"qualified immunity"** many police officers do not stand trial for many of their actions against citizen, as in the case of an African American first responder, Breonna Taylor, who was the victim of a killing by police during a "no knock warrant" search in her home in 2020. Black Lives Matter and other advocacy groups are questioning this policy. They are simply asking our nation legally to "defund the police." Pastor William Donnel Watley, prayed this prayer after reading his son, Matthew L. Watley's poem, "Death."

~Prayer~

"O God, when I first read the poem on death, I asked myself. Isn't this a strange subject for a young man to write about...Deaths are reported daily in the news. More personally, my son has seen

some of his peers buried. He has seen me as a pastor bury church members whom he has known most of his life. So death is a subject that he would reflect on....However, as I read his poem, I noticed his lack of fear and the hope of faith. I praise you for the hope that is ours as believers, the hope that now lives within the heart of my son. As a parent I pray that you would keep my children as they daily walk through mean streets. O God hold them in your hands. Keep them from hurt, harm, and danger and bless them with long life that they might glorify you and fulfill their potential. This my daily, heartfelt prayer that I lift before you. O God have mercy. In Jesus' name, amen."

Pastor Watley's prayer can be prayed for all of our children because God's promise to us is that *"the effectual, fervent prayer of a righteous man availeth much (James 5:16)."*

Voices

"Every day I pray for mankind
We're all slaves to a generation socialized, and sickness is in the mind
We are habitual thinkers, substance abusers and habitual drinkers
But free your mind because the plug is watching from the top floor
Hoping you too would fall for the illusions of a temporary

high
What we think we need to get by
But are we really trying when kids are dying and
depression is trending?
Are these the signs of an Armageddon?"
> *-H.E.R. (song lyrics "The Lord Is Coming")*

Day Twenty-One

Scripture:

"Evildoers do not understand what is right, but those who seek the LORD understand it full."

Proverbs 28:5

<u>Inspirational Commentary</u>

George Alexander McGuire (1866-1934) was a bishop and founder of the African Orthodox Church, as well as chaplain-general of the Universal Negro Improvement Association (UNIA). In 1913 during a strike and local riot by black workers in Antigua, McGuire was asked by British business owners and local religious leaders to help stop the activities of worker. McGuire did not. He advocated for fair wages and better living conditions for the workers. Upon his return to America, he joined Marcus Garvey and started the African Orthodox Church. On Good Friday, Bishop McGuire's prayer was:

~Prayer~

"Almighty Saviour, whose heavy Cross was laid upon the stalwart shoulders of Simon the Cyrenian, a son of Ham, in that sad hour of thine agony and mortal weakness, when the sons of Shem delivered thee into the hands of the sons Japheth to be

crucified, regard with thy favor this race still struggling beneath the cross of injustice, oppression, and wrong laid upon us by our persecutors. Strengthen us in our determination to free ourselves from their seat and exalt thou the humble and meek; through thy mercies and merits who livest and reignest with the Father and the Holy Ghost, world without end, Amen."

Voices

"My goodness. Y'all are interesting. Very interesting. You feeling good about yourself? You feel good about yourself? You feel good about yourself, don't you? For a failure to signal. . . Why am I being arrested? Can you tell me that part?" Sandra Bland

Day Twenty-Two

Scripture:

"His children are far from safety and included in their father's ruin. They are oppressed and crushed in the court of justice in the city's gat., And there is no one to rescue them."

Job 5:4

Inspirational Commentary

Elijah McClain (1996-2019) a 23-year-old massage therapist was stopped by police officers on August 24, 2019 because he had on a ski mask and was acting suspicious. He died after he was put in a choke hold by a police officer. According to the police video his last words were the following:

"I can't breathe. I have my ID right here. My name is Elijah McClain. That's my house. I was just going home. I'm an introvert. I'm just different. That's all. I'm so sorry. I have no gun. I don't do that stuff. I don't do any fighting. Why are you attacking me? I don't even kill flies! I don't eat meat! But I don't judge people, I don't judge people who do eat meat. Forgive me. All I was trying to do was become better. I will do it. I will do anything, sacrifice my identity, I'll do it. You all are phenomenal. You are beautiful and I love you. Try to forgive me. I'm a mood Gemini. I'm sorry. I'm so sorry.

Ow, that really hurt! You are all very strong. Teamwork makes the dream work. Oh, I'm sorry, I wasn't trying to do that. I just can't breathe correctly."

McClain's death in Denver was only months before we have the murder of George Floyd in Minnesota. Floyd's last words, "I can't breathe." Christians must remember these on-going injustices and pray. If we don't who will?

Voices

USA Today, "The price of just a few seconds lost: People." Andrew Redyk, 64 years old collapsed on the job. It took L.A. emergency service almost half an hour to reach him. He died.

Day Twenty-Three

Scripture:

"Therefore, confess your sins to each other and pray for each other so that you may be healed. The prayer of a righteous person is powerful and effective."

James 5:16

"You want something and do not have it; so you commit murder. And you covet something and cannot obtain it; so you engage in disputes and conflicts. You do not have, because you do not ask."

James 4:2

<u>Inspirational Commentary</u>

Malcolm X (1925-1965) is one of America's most controversial African American leader. Many people believed, like Ossie Davis, an African American actor and activist, in his eulogy to Malcom X, "…that he [Malcolm X] was our black manhood our black shining prince..." Malcolm X said.

~Prayer~

"I pray that God will bless everything that you do. I pray that you will grow intellectually so that you can understand the problems of the world and where you fit into in that world picture and I pray

that all the fear that has ever been in your heart will be taken out and when you look at that man you will know that he is nothing, but a coward and you won't fear him. Say Amen."

Malcolm X believed that African Americans needed justice in America and spoke out about how African Americans could obtain that justice. He also was a man of prayer. He was a man of action.

Voices

"Justice is what love looks like in public." Cornel West.

Day Twenty-Four

Scripture :

"Those who oppress the poor insult their Maker, but helping the poor honors him."

Proverbs 14:31

"A person who gets ahead by oppressing the poor or by showering gifts on the rich will end in poverty. Listen to the words of the wise; apply your heart to my instruction."

Proverbs 22:16-17

<u>Inspirational Commentary</u>

Rev. Albert Cleage (1911-2000) was the founder of the church of the Shrine of the Black Madonna. He was a black nationalist Christian minster, political candidate, and political organizer. He prayed in 1968, "A Prayer for African American Peoplehood."

~Prayer~

"Heavenly Father, we thank thee for the opportunity of coming into thy house. We thank thee for our new understanding of the teachings of thy Son, Jesus Christ. We thank thee foe knowledge that we are sustained and supported by thy strength and thy power. Be with us in everything we do in our efforts to unite and come together, in our efforts to

fight against the enemy who would destroy us. Be with us in the difficult task uniting and building a black brotherhood which has meaning in terms of today's world. We pray to thee with a sense of confidence in the future, the things which must be done, we will do. Sustain and support us as we go about our task. Amen."

The Shrine of the Black Madonna churches are in Atlanta, Houston, and Detroit, along with The Shrine of the Black Madonna Cultural Centers and bookstores. The Black Madonna is a depiction of the Virgin Mary with dark skin found in hundreds of Catholic churches throughout Europe. The importance of this icon cannot be underestimated as black advocacy groups throughout the United States are demanding the demolition of statues that have supported the legacy of slavery and racial oppression in America.

Voices

'Haven't Quite Shaken the Horror' said Howard Kester, after the Lynching of Claude Neal, a 23 years old farmhand.

Day Twenty-Five

Scripture:

Then Miriam and Aaron spoke against Moses because of the Ethiopian woman whom he had married; for he had married an Ethiopian woman. So they said, "Has the Lord indeed spoken only through Moses? Has He not spoken through us also?" And the Lord heard it. (Now the man Moses was very humble, more than all men who were on the face of the earth.) Suddenly the Lord said to Moses, Aaron, and Miriam, "Come out, you three, to the tabernacle of meeting!" So the three came out. Then the Lord came down in the pillar of cloud and stood in the door of the tabernacle and called Aaron and Miriam. And they both went forward. Then He said, "Hear now My words: If there is a prophet among you, I, the Lord, make Myself known to him in a vision; I speak to him in a dream. Not so with My servant Moses; He is faithful in all My house. I speak with him face to face, Even plainly, and not in dark sayings; And he sees the form of the Lord. Why then were you not afraid To speak against My servant Moses?" So the anger of the Lord was aroused against them, and He departed. And when the cloud departed from above the tabernacle, suddenly Miriam became leprous, as white as snow. Then Aaron turned toward Miriam, and there she was, a leper."

Numbers 12:1-10

<u>Inspirational Commentary</u>

Bloody Sunday (March 7, 1965), one of the two men who led this historic march across the Edmund Pettus Bridge to Selma, Alabama was Rep. John Lewis, whose body on July 26, 2020 laid in state for public viewing at the US Capitol in Washington, D. C. That during the nation's celebration of his legacy, John Lewis's body was carried across that bridge in Selma, Alabama for the last time as a memorial. News stations around the country spoke of his long fight for social justice and about his involvement on Bloody Sunday for voters' rights. Lewis and Hosea Williams marched across that bridge with 600 other marchers on Bloody Sunday. They were met by state troopers with Billy clubs, tear gas, and attacks to their body. They are among the courageous men and women who fought and have seen some changes in social justices but not the end of racism and violence against African Americans. The above scripture warns and encourages us about these dangers of racism.

Voices

"Three shots in the back. How do you justify that?" headlined the newspaper, when unarmed 17-year-old honor roll student, Antwon Rose II was fatally shot by an East Pittsburgh police officer on June 19, 2018.

Day Twenty-Six

Scripture:

*"The Lord said, "What have you done? The voice of your brother's [innocent] blood is crying out to Me from the ground [for **justice**]."*

Genesis 4:10

<u>Inspirational Commentary</u>

Hazel Scott (1920-1981) born in Trinidad, was a virtuosic jazz pianist, actress and singer whose life changed Race Relations in America, a televised 15-minute variety show that aired in 1950. According to Donald Bogle she was the first African American female to host. She was married to Adam Clayton Powell Jr., a renown U.S Representative from Harlem and a pastor of Abyssinian Baptist Church in New York. Her popularity predated the Civil Rights Movement, but she was not exempt from Jim Crow segregation. She created her own style to fight racial degradation and oppression. She had a deep understanding of God in her life. According to Adam, her husband, Hazel had in her life one of the greatest acts of faith I have ever seen. One morning, accompanied by Mabel, Hazel went to Notre Dame, got down on her knees in front of the altar, and vowed she would not move until God gave her strength. She stayed there until her knees actually became bloody. When she finally did rise to her feet, she had the power and strength and the faith to never again touch or desire a drop of alcohol. She became an exceptionally religious person.

Chilton, Scott's biographer, noted that she was not a heavy drinker but the above occurred during a period in Scott's life when she wanted cleansing and searched for meaning. Chilton included the following prayer of Scott:

~Prayer~

"Soul of Christ sanctify me. Body of Christ save me. Blood of Christ inebriate me. Water from Christ's side wash me. Passion of Christ strengthen me. O good Jesus, hear me. Within Thy wounds hide me. Suffer me not to be separated from thee. From the malicious enemy, defend me. In the hour of my death, call me. And bid me come unto thee. That I may praise thee with thy saints and with thy angels. Forever and ever. Amen."

Her many contributions and strength to live a life that produced continuous racial uplift can be seen in her faith and prayers.

Voices

"Latasha Harlins, remember that name... Cause a bottle of juice is not something to die for" ... "Something 2 Die 4,"

Tupac Shakur. Latasha Harlins 15-years-old fatally shot in 1994 by Soon Ja Du.

Day Twenty-Seven

Scripture:

"When justice is done, it is a joy to the righteous but terror to evildoers."

Proverbs 21:15 (ESV)

<u>Inspirational Commentary</u>

Paul Cuffee, (1759-1817) was born free in Massachusetts and was an entrepreneur. He was a black millionaire. In the 1800's he led the first Back-to-Africa effort. His work paved the way for the African Colonization Society. He was a devoted Christian, and regularly taught at Westport Massachusetts and believed in a multi-racial society. His father, Cuffee Solum an Ashanti born in Africa, as a child was brought to Rhode Island and sold into slavery. He was given his freedom in 1754. Cuffee Solum worked hard and purchased land. He married and Ruth Moses, a Native American Wampanoag, had ten children. A Black Quaker, Paul Cuffee founded in Westport, Massachusetts the first racially integrated school in North America. He was instrumental in helping nine free African American families to settle in Sierra Lona on his trip in 1812. He has been perceived by his biographers as an extraordinary man. He has been quoted as saying, "My soul feels free to travel for the welfare of my fellow creatures both here and hereafter."

Many devoted Christians like Cuffee, have embraced their times with a compassion and fervor to end the dehumanization of African people. My question is how and why this present generation of Christian passivity to directly confront these issues in at least corporate prayer is neglected?

Voices

"One thing I'm here to say is I'm proud to be a Black young man." Caleb Reed was a 17-year-old Freedom Fighter who wanted #CopsOutCPS. Officers found Reed lying on a sidewalk about 1 p.m. Friday in the 1900 block of West Granville Avenue in Cook County.

Day Twenty-Eight

Scripture:

"And He told them a parable to the effect that they ought to always pray and not lose heart. He said, "In a certain city there was a judge who neither feared God nor respected man. And there was a widow in that city who kept coming to him and saying, 'Give me justice against my adversary.' For a while he refused, but afterward he said to himself, 'Though I neither fear God nor respect man, yet because this widow keeps bothering me, I will give her justice, so that she will not beat me down by her continual coming.'"

Luke 18:1-8

Inspirational Commentary

Nimrod was a descendant of Cush, a Cushite Black. Although he was real his historical period is hard to determine. Biblically Nimrod was described in Genesis 10:9 as a "mighty hunter before the Lord." According to Rev. Walter Arthur McCray

> *"He [Nimrod] served as a protector of the community. He was ipso facto the representative head who was a social activist. Nimrod's deliverance of the community preceded his ascension to kingship in a like manner to that of the Judges of Israel who ascended into their offices by virtue of their acts of deliverance performed on*

behalf of their oppressed people. Biblical scholars…attach an "evilness" and "militarism" that would be better be applied historically to racist European people who over the face of this globe have always sought to conquer, colonize, and oppress Black and non-white peoples."

It is sad, like the recent reference made by President Clinton about Stokely Carmichael in his speech during John Lewis's funeral, that outsiders of the culture feel that they can defame African American leaders who fight for their community "by any means necessary." We appreciate our biblical scholars like Rev. McCray who corrects these distortions and has placed Nimrod into his historical and cultural context to understand God's greatest and the greatness of the Bible.

Voices

"Sir, you're trying to steal my car and you're telling me that if I don't get out of my car you are gonna kidnap me and probably planning on kidnapping my kids too. Listen, if you plan on shooting somebody today, you will probably get your wish. . . When you put your hands on me. You will have to murder me. You will have to kill me. I promise you! . . . (To another officer) Sir, I am in the middle of suing the government." Korryn Gaines…Traffic Stop tape

Day Twenty-Nine

Scripture:

The small and great are there; and the servant is free from his master.

Job 3:19

The [boundary] lines [of the land] have fallen for me in pleasant places; Indeed, my heritage is beautiful to me.

Psalm 16:6

Inspirational Commentary

Sarah Mapps Douglass (1806-1882) was an early African American teacher, abolitionist and founder of several women's literary and antislavery organizations. She was born free to parents, Robert Douglass and Grace Bustill Douglass, who were also abolitionists in Philadelphia.

"But while I thus repose, as under my own vine and fig tree, my heart is filled with sorrow for my enslaved sisters. The Sabbath is no day of rest to the poor slave—she hears no hymn, no prayer, upon this holy morning. She has no Bible in which to read the matchless love of Jesus. Alas! She has never been taught to read: no ray of light penetrates the darkness of her mental vision. Sister slave, fainting with toil and sickness in the burning sun, cheer up! Christ is near thee, even in thy heart! Seek Him—He will be found of thee—He has undertaken they cause—He will plead with thy oppressors Himself. 'Call upon Him from amidst thy bonds, for assuredly He will hear thee.' Cheer up—a few of the noblest and best of thy countrywomen have acknowledged that thou are their sister: the time of thy deliverance draweth nigh. The time is approaching when Christ shall reign king of nations: then look to him alone. He hears thy sighs and counts thy tears He shall lift up thy head." The sounds of the church bell now broke the stillness of the morning, and Ella arose and went forth to the Sophanisba Philadelphia. According to Aijuan she may have been the first Black woman to publicly address an audience on slavery.

Voices

A 3 second Dashcam video report, "Police!" (Two Shots fired) Yvette Smith down. Deputy Daniel Adams later charged with murder.

Day Thirty

Scripture:

"His descendants will be powerful on earth; the godly will be blessed"

Psalm 112:2

"There they are, overwhelmed with dread, for God is in the company of the righteous."

Psalm 14:5

<u>Inspirational Commentary</u>

Moms for Black Lives Matter begin with George Zimmerman, the officer that shot Trayvon Martin. It was birth from women whose children's lives had been interrupted through violence. Mothers who also need to stop their children from being demonized but seen as the beautiful people they were. They are changing the nation's narrative about the sons and daughters of African Americans. Reading the history books, listen to media, we understand that the humanizing African Americans in this country is a continuous and uphill battle. I applaud theses mothers for their courage and tirelessness in this struggle and their struggle for justice for their loved ones. Our prayer can continuously be not to look out for my four and no more. Our prayer can coincide with Dr. Martin Luther King's. He asked that we look at the content of the character of each other. Not just the small percentage of

African American lawyers, doctors, nurses, and other professionals but every African American man, woman, and child as a valuable contribution to our "beloved community."

Voices

"I guess he felt that I just was angry and mad and just hated him," Sutton continued. "I said that's too much energy to give you, I don't want to waste that energy on building something negative. Instead ... I'm going to build something positive." Sutton is the brother of Rekia Boyd speaking about ex- police officer Servin who pulled a gun, stuck it out of the window of his car and fired into a group, hitting 22-year-old Rekia Boyd in the head. She was instantly killed.

Epilogue

My hope is that many will consistently and fervently ask for Black Lives to Matter as God commands in Leviticus 26:8, "Five of you shall chase a hundred, and a hundred of you shall chase ten thousand, and your enemies shall fall before you by the sword." Never cease to pray for the liberation of African Americans
according to Lamentations 3:49-50, "My eyes will flow unceasingly, without relief, until the Lord looks down from heaven and sees."

Thank you for joining me in prayer. God will move because we have asked according to His word.

Bibliography

Ajuan Maria Mance. *Before Harlem: An Anthology of African American Literature from the Long Nineteenth Century*. Vol. First edition, Univ Tennessee Press, 2016.

Bradford, Hopkins Sarah. *Harriet, The Moses of Her People*. Geo. R. Lockwood and Son, *1886.*

Brooks, Maegan Parker. *A Voice That Could Stir an Army: Fannie Lou Hamer and the Rhetoric of the Black Freedom Movement*, University Press of Mississippi, 2014.

ProQuest Ebook Central, http://ebookcentral.proquest.com/lib/emich/detail.action?docID=1701947. Created from emich on 2020-08-18 20:13:07.

Chilton, Karen. *Hazel Scott: The Pioneering Journey of a Jazz Pianist, From Café Society to Hollywood to HUAC.* E-book, Ann Arbor, MI: University of Michigan Press,2008, https://doiorg.ezproxy.emich.edu/10.3998/mpub.197245. Accessed 26 Jun 2020.

Chisholm, Shirley, *1924-2005. Unbought And Unbossed.* Boston: Houghton Mifflin, 1970.

Tutu Bishop Desmond , speech, 1985.Quoted in *Equality*, Volume 1, Issue 1, 1989 https://sojo.net/articles/12-sayings-desmond-tutu-voice-justice-time-division. Accessed 13 July 2020.

Cuffee, Paul. Letter, Westport (February 22, 1813).https://libquotes.com/paul-cuffee/quote/lbf5q1q Accessed August 17, 2020.

Delany, M. *Martin R. Delany: a documentary reader*. University of North Carolina Press. 2003

DeSantis, Marissa. https://www.standard.co.uk/insider/alist/who-shirley-chisolm-mrs-america-real-story-a4492676.html. Accessed 8 July 2020.

Fyfe, Christopher. "Captain Paul Cuffe's Logs and Letters, 1808–1817: A Black Quaker's 'Voice from within the Veil' . Edited by Rosalind Cobb Wiggins. Washington, DC: Howard University Press, 1996. Pp. xxi+529. (ISBN 0-88258-183-X)." *The Journal of African History* 39.1 (1998): 147-174. 18 8 2020. <http://journals.cambridge.org/abstract_s00 21853797397163>.

Hogan, Wesley. "The Speeches of Fannie Lou Hamer: To Tell It like It Is." *Journal of Southern History* 78.3 (2012): 775. 18 8 2020.<https://questia.com/library/journal/1 1-300443483/the-speeches-of-fannie-lou hamer-to-tell-it-like>.

King, Martin Luther, Jr. Ph.D. *"Thou, Dear God": Prayers That Open Hearts and Spirits*. ed. Baldwin Lewis. Beacon Press, 2011.

McCray, Walter Arthur. *The Black Presence in the Bible and the Table of Nations. Black Light Fellowship*,1990.

Mack, Dwayne. "Hazel Scott: A Career Curtailed." *Journal of African American History* 91.2 (2006): 153. 18 8 2020. <https://journals.uchicago.edu/doi/abs/10.1 86/jaahv91n2p153>.

Mills, Hay. *This Little Light of Mine*, Fannie Lou Hammer ch. 8, (1993).

Malcolm https://slife.org/malcolm-xs-prayers/. Accessed 24 July 2020.

Pearman, Eric G. *"The Least of these": Ida B. Wells - Barnett's Intraracial Critique of African-American Clergy and Lay Leadership*, ProQuest Dissertations Publishing, 2002.

Peter Marshall and David Manuel. *Sounding Forth the Trumpet: 1837-1860* by, p. 358

ProQuest Ebook Central, http://ebookcentral.proquest.com/lib/emich/detail.action?do cID=1701947.

Created from emich on 2020-08-19 06:23:28.

Excerpt of of "Korryn Gaines Traffic Stop," *YouTube*, accessed March 19, 2017, https://www-youtube-com.ezproxy.emich.edu/watch?v=Zriy1N2hLxM Traffic

Stop," *YouTube*, accessed March 19, 2017, https://www-youtube-com.ezproxy.emich.edu/watch?v=Zriy1N2hLxM

The Eyes on the Prize Civil Rights Reader: documents, speeches and firsthand accounts from the Black Freedom Struggle, 1954–1990, ed. Clayborne Carson et al. (Penguin Books, 1991, p. 121.

Walker, David, 1785-1830, "Walker's Appeal, in Four Articles: Together with a Preamble, to the Coloured Citizens of the World, but in Particular, and Very Expressly, to Those of the United States of America, Written in Boston,

Washington, Margaret. *Sojourner Truth's America.* E-book, Urbana: University of Illinois Press, 2009, https://hdl-handle net.ezproxy.emich.edu/2027/heb.09319. Accessed 26 Jun 2020.

State of Massachusetts, September 28, 1829," *Black Self-Publishing*, accessed June 30,2020, https://www.americanantiquarian.org/blackpublishing/items/show/11045.

Zoe Spencer, Olivia N. Perlow; Sassy Mouths, Unfettered Spirits, and the Neo-Lynching of Korryn Gaines and Sandra Bland: Conceptualizing Post Traumatic Slave Master Syndrome and the Familiar "Policing" of Black Women's Resistance in Twenty-First-Century America. *Meridians* 1 September 2018; 17 (1): 163–183. doi:

https://doiorg.ezproxy.emich.edu/10.1215/1536693669551
75

https://www.cbc.ca/news/world/elijah-mcclain-police-
photos-1.5637074. Accessed 25 August 2020.
https://en.wikipedia.org/wiki/Death_of_Elijah_McClain.
Accessed 25 August 2020.

https://www.beliefnet.com/faiths/prayer/2009/01/prayers-
from-african-americans-in-history.aspx. Date June 21,
2020

https://en.wikiquote.org/wiki/Martin_Delany. Date
accessed June 29, 2020

https://en.wikipedia.org/wiki/Paul_Cuffe Date accessed:
August 17, 2020.

https://time.com/4446349/nat-turner-rebellion-history. Date
accessed: June 23,2020

https://en.wikiquote.org/wiki/Ida_B._Wells. Date accessed:
June 23, 2020.

https://en.wikipedia.org/wiki/London_Ferrill. Date
accessed June 29, 2020

https://ellabakercenter.org/blog/2013/12/ellas-song-we-
who-believe-in-freedom-cannot-rest-until-it-comes.
Accessed June 24, 2020.
https://www.google.com/search?q=her+the+lord+is+comin
g&oq=Her+the+&aqs=chrome.5.0j46l3j69i57j0j46j0.1586

6j0j8&sourceid=chrome&ie=UTF-8. Accessed 25 July 2020.

https://chicago.suntimes.com/crime/2020/8/2/21352065/caleb-reed-dies-west-rogers-park-shooting-granville-granvill. *Access: 4 August 2020*

Excerpt of "Sandra Bland Traffic Stop (Raw Uncut)," *YouTube*, July 10, 2015, https://www.youtube.com.ezproxy.emich.edu/watch?v=URAZ3umt7v0&t=766s

Cover and Artwork Designed by:
Yusuf Dubois Davis Abdul Lateef

b1977
Yusuflateef.com
yusuflateef77@gmail.com
Education - Bowling Green State University - MFA /
Columbus College of Art and Design -BFA

• Toledo School for the Arts instructor - Intro-Foundations
Visual Arts

• Adjunct Professor - University of Toledo School of
Visual Arts

• Radiant City Arts - Co-Founder - a for-profit collective
focused on bringing quality
programming to communities and institutions for the
enhancement of lives through the creative process.

• Youth Arts Alliance.
/youthartsalliance.com - Artist Facilitator for Juvenile
detention
centers in, Monroe / Ypsilanti Michigan

• Co-founder of the Toledo Black Artist Coalition

Yusuf Lateef utilizes visual art principles as vehicles for
realizing the potential for growth in our everyday lives. As
an artist, Lateef looks at common experiences as something
transformative while working to imagine the physicality of
an "undefended space/life" through community
engagement as art practice.

About the Author

Dr. Imelda Hunt has taught African American studies courses for more than twenty-five years. She holds a Ph.D. in American Culture from Bowling Green State University, with a major in African American Culture and Black Popular Culture. She also holds master's degrees in African American Theatre and American Culture, with an emphasis in African American Culture, from Bowling Green State University. She earned a bachelor's degree in education and communication from the University of Toledo.

Dr. Hunt is the founder of New Works Writers Series, a black theater and arts organization whose accomplishments include the first major poetry slam competition in northwest Ohio and dozens of productions, readings and workshops presented at venues like the Toledo Museum of Art and the Charles H. Wright Museum of African American History in Detroit, Michigan. She has been the recipient of several National Endowment for the Humanities summer seminars grants.

In 2015 the City of Toledo recognized Dr. Hunt for many years of producing and directing plays inspired by black artists and authors in the community. She is a noted poet and has been published in many anthologies including, *The Glass Review* and the Toledo Arts Commission's Sidewalk Poetry.

She is also the recipient of many other awards for her scholarship and artistic talents. She currently attends worship services at The Worship Center in Toledo, Ohio under the leadership of Bishop Pastor Patricia McKinstry. During her tenure at Worship Center, she has been a faithful member of the tape ministry, the hospitality ministry, and the college ministry. She accepted Christ as a child and rededicated her life to Him in 1987.

Her other published books include:

Black Culture Traditions: Visible and Invisible. Cognella Academic Publishing: California, 2019

The History of Art Tatum, 19010-1932. ASA Publishing Corporation: Michigan, 2018

Does a Genius: A Tribute to Art Tatum. ASA Publishing Corporation: Michigan, 2017.

~ Yusuf Dubois Davis Abdul Lateef~

9 798594 134928